The Double Search

Studies in Atonement and Prayer

THE

DOUBLE SEARCH

STUDIES IN

ATONEMENT AND PRAYER

BY

RUFUS M. JONES, A.M., Litt.D.

Professor of Philosophy in Haverford College

FRIENDS
UNITED
PRESS

RICHMOND
INDIANA

Library of Congress Cataloging in Publication Data

Jones, Rufus Matthew, 1863-1948.
  The double search.

  Reprint of the 1906 ed. published by J.C. Winston,
Philadelphia.
  1. Atonement.   2. Prayer.   I. Title.
BT265.j6   1975   248'.3   75-14316
ISBN O-913408-18-2

CONTENTS

5

FOREWORD

This book was written during 1905, the year of John Wilhelm Rowntree's death, as lectures for a Summer School in Street, Somerset, England. That Summer School was memorable, for those attending were profoundly conscious of their leader's loss. They were, also, filled with the high purpose of taking up and carrying on the work which John Wilhelm Rowntree had been dedicated.

A number of people have expressed an interest in having the book back in print, hence this edition, seventy years after it was first written. We trust it will serve a valuable purpose.

Earl J. Prignitz

"We are always gathered around the Divine Centre of our being; and, indeed, if we could withdraw from it, our being would at once be dissolved away, and we should cease to exist at all. But, near as it is to us, often we do not direct our eyes to it. When, however, we do so direct our gaze, we attain to the end of our desires and to the rest of our souls, and our song is no more a discord, but, circling round our Centre, we pour forth a divinely inspired chorale. And in the choral dance we behold the source of our life, the fountain of our intelligence, the primal good, *the root of the soul.*"

Plotinus, Ennead VI.

8

INTRODUCTION.

THERE is a famous myth in Plato's Symposium told to explain the origin of love. This myth says that primitive man was round, and had four hands and four feet, and one head with two faces looking opposite ways. He could walk on his legs if he liked, But he also could roll over and over with great speed if he wished to go anywhere very fast.

Because of their fleetness and skill these "Round people" were dangerous rivals in power to Zeus himself and he adopted the plan of weakening them by cutting each one of them in two. In remembrance of the original undivided state each half, ever since unsatisfied and alone, seeks eagerly for the other half. Each human being is thus a half — a tally — and love is the longing to be united. The two halves are seeking to be joined again in the original whole. Such in briefest compass is the myth.

But as the dialogue advances love is traced to a higher source. It is discovered to be a passion for the eternal, a passion which rises in the soul at the sight of an object which suggests the eternal, from which the soul has come into the temporal. The soul is alien here and its chief joy in the midst of the shows of sense is joy at the sight of something which reminds it of its old divine home. Thus, again, Plato tells us that love has its birth in the division

of what was once a whole. We yearn
for that from which we have come.

> " Though inland far we be
> Our souls have sight of that immortal
>   sea
>   That brought us hither."

We may ignorantly stop at some mid-
way good and miss the homeward path,
but our real search, our master passion,
is for that divine Other to whom we
belong. So at last Plato poetizes.

We have discovered through other
lips, what he could not tell us, that the
search is a double search. We have
learned that the Divine Other whom we
seek is also seeking us. The myth, told
at the beginning, is more suggestive than
it seemed. It may perhaps do for a
parable of the finite and the Infinite, the

soul and its Father.   May they not once
have been in union?   May not our birth
in time be a drawing away into individ-
uality from the Divine whole?   And
then may not the goal of the entire
drama of personal life be the restoration
of that union on a higher spiritual level?
May it not be, that we are never again
to fuse the skirts of self and merge into
a union of oblivion, but rather that we
are to rise to a love-union in which His
will becomes our will — a union of conscious cooperation?   So at any rate I believe.   But this little book is not a book
of speculation.   It is not written to urge
some fond belief.

We have learned, I say, that life reveals a double search.   Man's search for
God is as plain a fact as his search for
food.   He has, beyond question, blun-

dered at it and frequently missed the trail, but that man in all lands and in all times has maintained some kind of search for an invisible Companion is a momentous fact.

The other half of the story is, I think, still more momentous. It is full of pathos and tragedy, but laden with the prophecy of final triumph. I have tried to tell again this story, surely an old, old story, but always needing to be retold in the current language and the prevailing conceptions of the time. The main feature of this book is its insistence on the facts of experience. Its terms are not those of theology, but those of life, or if I have used theological words I have endeavored to re-vitalize them. I shall assume that my readers are familiar with the idea of the *conjunct life* which

I have expounded at length in a former book.[1]   It is now well known that " isolated " personality is impossible.   He who is to enjoy the rights and privileges of personality must be conjunct with others.   He must be an organic member in a social group, and share himself with his fellows, while at the same time he receives contributions from them.   This principle of the conjunct life reaches beyond the finite social fellowship in which a man forms and expresses his personality.   God and man are conjunct.   The ground for this position will not be gone over here.   It has been sufficiently presented elsewhere.

I believe, however, that no psychological discovery has ever thrown so

[1] " Social Law in the Spiritual World," Philadelphia, 1904.

much light upon the meaning of atonement and prayer as this fact of the conjunct life does, and I hope that many
others may come to feel the freshness
and reality of these deepest religious
truths as I have felt them.

In touching these two subjects we are
touching the very pillars of religion. If
atonement — God's search for us —
and prayer — our search for Him —
are not real, then religion has no permanent ground of reality. But there
can be no question that our age has witnessed a serious weakening of faith in
both these central aspects of religion.
The doctrine of the atonement does not
grip men as it did once, and there are
persons all about us who are perplexed
about the place and efficacy of prayer.
It is no frivolous questioning. It is not

the result of a lazy attitude of mind. It is stern and serious. There is only one way to change this condition. We must make men feel again the reality of the atonement and the reality of prayer. That is the task which lies before those of us who believe. The day for dogmatic assertion is past. It rolls off most minds now as water rolls from oiled silk. The truths which march with power are the truths which are verified by, and buttressed with, facts. We must, then, learn how to carry the laboratory method into our religious teaching and ground our message in actual reality.

This slender book is an attempt to approach these two subjects — atonement and prayer — in this spirit and by this method. We can never get the telescope or microscope turned upon the objects of spiritual experience and we cannot use the mathematical method which has worked such wonders in the physical realm. There will always be some who cannot *see* the evidence. But it is worth while to show that these two pillars of religion do rest — not on air — but on experience which can be verified and tested; that they rest in fact on the elemental basis of life, upon which we live our common social life together.

I trust it will help some to find the trail, and that it will convince some perplexed, though honest, readers that however their own quest has fared there is another search beside their own,— the quest of a Divine Companion who spares no pain or cost to bring us all into a fellowship with Him.

Haverford, Pennsylvania,
New Year 1906.

The Historical and the Inward Christ

"All who since Jesus have come into union with God have come into union with God *through Him.* And thus it is confirmed in every way that, even to the end of time, all wise and intelligent men must bow themselves reverently before this Jesus of Nazareth; and that the more wise, intelligent and noble they themselves are, the more humbly will they recognize the exceeding nobleness of this great and glorious manifestation of the Divine Life."

Fichte's " Way Toward the Blessed Life," p. 391.

"Christ is the Eternal Humanity in the life of the Infinite."

George A. Gordon's " The Christ of Today," p. 136.

"The word of God is continually born anew in the hearts of holy men."

Epistle to Diognetus, A. D. 125.

THE HISTORICAL AND THE
INWARD CHRIST.

THERE was once a widespread fear that exact methods of historical research would deprive us of that luminous divine Figure toward whom the world had reverently turned its face for more than eighteen centuries. Some suspected that our records of His life were crowded with myth and legend, others believed that the singular story which had so profoundly touched the world's heart was the creation of highly wrought enthusiastic disciples. Today, after more than half a century of critical sifting and acute probing, this luminous Life is more firmly established as the central fact of history than ever before.

" That one Face, far from vanish, rather
     grows
Or decomposes but to recompose
Becomes my universe which loves and
     knows."

It is not my purpose at present to retell the story, or to point out how much criticism has left unshaken. I want rather to show how the historical Christ, as a revelation of God, fits into a cosmic system of evolution and how He is related to the Spirit that witnesses with our spirits and is the inward life of the Saints of all ages and lands.

I shall not use the language or the methods of theology. I shall feel my way along the great arteries of human experience and try to throw light and suggestion rather than to establish some final and complete dogma. To begin at once with the problem before us, how shall we think of Christ? Was He man? Was He God? Was He some miraculous union of two essentially unrelated natures? Here are the questions which have split the Christian world up into camps and which have busied schoolmen in all the centuries.

The difficulty in almost all the theological discussions on the subject has been that they started with God and man isolated, separated, unrelated. No true revelation of such a God ever could be made through a human life, for divinity and humanity on this theory are conceived as two totally diverse natures. Modern psychology and recent studies of social life have made us familiar with a deeper view of human personality and have prepared for a more adequate study of Divine personality than was possible when the historic creeds were formulated. We know that God and man are *conjunct* and that neither can be separated absolutely from the other. There never has been any doubt of man's need of God, but we now know that God also needs us and that our lives are mutually organic. Every clew which leads us to God shows Him to us as a spiritual and social Being — in no sense solitary and self-sufficient. Our own self-consciousness, our own ideals, our passion for the unrealized, imply and involve more than an impersonal energy at the heart of things. There must be a spiritual matrix for this living, throbbing, growing social organism in which personal life is formed. Our own experience carries in itself the implication of a genuinely spiritual Person at the heart of the universe of whom we all partake. The spiritual history of the race has forever settled this elemental fact, at least for all who feel the full significance of life. It is not an assumption, it is not a mere belief — it is involved in all we feel and know and are. But a spiritual, personal Being must reveal Himself. An unmanifested God — unknown and unknowable — is no God at all. He would be abstract and unreal. The least human person who poured his life out into those about him — who loved and suffered for the sake of another — would be a higher being than an infinite God shut up in the closed circle of His own self life. It is

a law as old as the morning star that
one must lose himself to find himself,
must give to get, must go forth bearing
precious seed in order to come again
with sheaves of harvest. The moment
it is settled that there is a divine Person as the ultimate reality of the universe,
it is also settled that He will reveal Himself, that He will put His Life into
manifold manifestations and that He
will find His joy in " working all things
up to better," to use Clement's phrase.

So long as the processes of evolution
were confined to the plant and brute there
could be no revelation of anything but
force; or at most there could be only
dawnings of anything higher. The
forms of life which won in the struggle
and survived were manifestations of
power — they hardly implied anything

more. The tough spine and the strong jaw and the sharp claw were all that mattered. Everything that appeared was pushed into existence by a force from behind. There was no sign or hint of freedom, or of life formed under the sway of a vision or an ideal. Things moved " for a million aeons through the vast, waste dawn " toward a goal, but the goal was never in sight and it played no part in the process.

John Fiske has, somewhere, denied the truth of the proverb that " nature abhors leaps," and he has given a beautiful illustration from the cutting of a cone. If you pass a plane parallel to the base of a cone you cut a circle. If you tilt the plane slightly the curve becomes an ellipse. The ellipse grows more eccentric as the tilting increases and finally without any warning your plane cuts a parabola whose sides curve off into infinity and never touch ends again. Some such mighty leap appears in the process of evolution. Up to a certain point life evolved by forces working *a tergo*.[1] There is a slight tilt in the system and a being appears capable of selecting a goal for himself and of acting to attain it, a being who could live in some degree for a world as it ought to be.[2]

This is what in America we call "the great divide"—the watershed which determines the streams of a continent. As soon as there was a being who could

[1] The term *a tergo* causation means that what happens is produced entirely by the push or the pull of forces. There is an exact equation — the antecedent *determines* the consequent.

[2] It is not true, of course, that there is an absolute "break" in the upward processes of life. Even in the lower forms of life there are hints of

select ideals and live for conscious ends a new kind of evolution began. The other side of " the divide," evolution had been physical,— body, and body function had been the goal. This side " the divide," it was spiritual and social, and the goal was the evolution of the man within man. The things which mattered now were love, sacrifice, service, goodwill rather than " tooth and claw." Before, nature's goal had been along the line of least resistance. Now, the line of march set straight against instinct and along the line of greatest resistance. There could be advance on

higher possibilities. There is an elemental struggle for the life of others which has in it the potentiality of love and sacrifice. But there is no " sign " on the lower levels — before self-consciousness dawned — of any capacity for an ideal, or of *any power to develop by the forecast and vision of the goal.*

this side " the divide," only as the ideal became clearer and its sway more coercive.

Ever since man was man he has transcended the actual and lived by vision, which means, I think, that finite and infinite are not sundered and that we always partake of more than just ourselves. Beyond the edge of what we are there is always dawning a farther possibility — that which we ought to be — the *a fronte* compulsion.[1]   This is one of God's ways of revealing Himself.   It is a man's chief glory — the glory of the imperfect.

" Growth came when, looking your last
on them all

---

[1] The term *a fronte* compulsion means the compelling power of an ideal which influences by an attraction from in front.

You turned your eyes inwardly one fine
    day
And cried with a start — what if we so
    small
Be greater and grander the while than
    they?
Are they perfect of lineament, perfect of
    stature?
In both, of such lower types are we
Precisely because of our wider nature;
For time, theirs — ours, for eternity.
Today's brief passion limits their range;
It seethes with the morrow for us and
    more.
They are perfect — how else? They
    shall never change.
We are faulty — why not? We have
    time in store." [1]

[1] Browning's "Old Pictures in Florence."

This slow unveiling of the ideal, of the goal, is, I believe, the divine method of making man, and it makes us feel at once how nearer than near God is and how all the way on and up He is in the very tissue and fabric of our lives — no foreign creator who moulded us out of clay and left us to run, or to run down, like a clock.

For centuries man won his slender spiritual victories, cultivated his rugged virtues, sloughed off some marks of ape and tiger and formed habits of altruism under the influence of ideals which the highest personal types of the race revealed. These types of men were focus points, manifesting in some feeble measure the ultimate reality and casting out hints of the line of march. Sometimes they were conscious that they were or-

gans of a larger Life which used them,
sometimes they were girded, like Cyrus,
for a divine mission, though they knew
not Him whom they served. Thus the
unbroken revelation of the infinite was
slowly made, as the age could bear it —
" God spake at sundry times and in di-
vers manners."

Strangely enough the loftiest men of
the pre-Christian period were always
vaguely or dimly forecasting a diviner
life than any ordinary type of man revealed. The human heart was always
groping for an unveiling of God which
would set the race to living on a new
level. This longing rose among the Hebrews to a steady passion which burned
brighter as the clouds in their national
sky grew blacker. There was a Christ
ideal centuries before Christ actually

came in the flesh, though this ideal was always deeply tinged and colored by the age which gave it birth. But even so, it lighted the sky of the future and gave many a man heart and hope through long periods of dreary pessimism. When lo, a tilting of the plane, and the ellipse becomes a parabola with infinite stretch of curve!

" In fullness of time God sent forth His Son." How shall we think of Jesus that is called the Christ? Speaking first in the terms of evolution, *I* think of Him as the type and goal of the race — the new Adam, the spiritual norm and pattern, the Son of Man who is a revelation of what man at his height and full stature is meant to be; and this is the way Paul thought of Him: " Till *we all* come in the unity of the faith, and of the knowledge of the Son of God, unto a perfect man, unto the measure of the stature of the fullness of Christ." Eph. IV, 13. "Whom he did foreknow, he did predestinate to be conformed to the image of his Son that *He* might be the first born among many brethren." Rom. VIII, 29. "The expectation of the whole creation is waiting for the manifestation of sons of God." Rom. VIII, 19.

The actual fact is that this Life has, profoundly or remotely, touched every personal life in Europe for a thousand years and has been the goal and standard for all aspiring souls. He is the pattern in the mount, the *a fronte* force which has drawn the individual and the race steadily up to their higher destiny. On the spiritual side of "the great divide" the goal is in sight and the goal is an efficient factor in the process of the evolution of the man within man.

But this pattern-aspect of the Christ life is only one aspect, and we must not raise it out of due balance and perspective. *Christ is God humanly revealed.* As soon as we realize that personality is always a revelation of the ultimate reality of the universe there are no metaphysical difficulties· in the way of an actual incarnation of God. It is rather what one would expect. There is no other conceivable way in which God could be revealed to man. If He is a personal being; if He is love and tenderness and sympathy, and not mere force, only a Person can show Him. And if we are not kindred in nature, if we have not something in common, in a word if we are not *conjunct,* then it is hard to see how any revelation of Him could be made which would mean anything to us. But if we are *conjunct,* as our own self-consciousness implies, then an incarnation, a complete manifestation in Personality, or as Paul puts it, " in the face of Jesus Christ," is merely the crown and pinnacle of the whole divine process.

If we are wise we shall not bother ourselves too much over the metaphysical puzzles which the schoolmen have formulated. We no longer have the puzzle which was so urgent with them, how two natures, pole-wide apart, could be united in one Person, for we now know that divinity and humanity are not pole-wide apart. There is something human in God and something divine in man and they belong together.

We shall not, again, be over-anxious about the question of nativity. Note the grandeur and the simplicity of Paul's text about it: "God sent forth His Son born of a woman," and there he stops with no attempt to furnish details. John is equally lofty: "The Word became flesh and dwelt among us and we beheld His glory." There is no appeal to curiosity. There is no syllable about the *how*. Two synoptic gospels have given us a simple story of the nativity which has profoundly impressed men in all ages and which will always appeal to the deepest instincts in us. But the *method* of Christ's coming, embodied in these two accounts, must not be forced. The devout soul must be free, as both Paul and John were free, to leave the *how* wrapped in mystery. That He came out of our humanity we shall always believe. That He came down out of the highest divinity we shall equally believe. That He was a babe and increased in wisdom, that He learned as He grew, that He was tempted and learned through temptation, are all necessary steps, for there is no other path to spiritual Personality and He must have been " made perfect through sufferings," or He could not have been the Captain of salvation.

Speculations and dogmas have taken men's thoughts away from verifiable facts. Here was a life which settled forever that the ultimate reality is Love. He brought into focus, or rather He wove into the living tissue of a personal life, the qualities of character which belong to an infinitely good being and with quiet simplicity He said, "If you see me you see the Father."

I have spoken, perhaps, as though the revelation of the human goal, and the unveiling of the divine Character were two different things. Christ does both, but both are one. If you bring a diamond into the light you occasion a double revelation. There is a revelation of the glorious beauty of the jewel. While it lay in the dark you never knew its possibilities. It was easily mistaken for a piece of glass. Now it flashes and burns and reveals itself because it has found the element for which it was meant. But there is also at the same time a revelation of the mystery of light. You discover now new wonders and new glories in light itself. Most objects absorb part of its rays and imperfectly transmit it to the eye.   Here is an object which tells you its real nature.   Now you see it as it is.   So Christ shows us at once man and God.   In a definite historic setting and in the limitations of a concrete personal life, Christ has unveiled the divine nature and taught us to say " Father " and He has, in doing that, showed us the goal and type of human life.   The Son of God and the Son of Man is one person.

Now comes our second question how shall we think of the inward, the spiritual, the eternal Christ?   The first interpreters, notably Paul and John, early in their experience, came to think of Christ as a cosmic Being.   They read the universe in the light of His revelation and soon used His name to name the entire manifestation of God: " In Him," says

Paul, " all things consist." " All things were made by Him," says John, " and without Him was not anything made that was made. In Him was life and the life was the light of men." John 1, 2, 3. It was through Him that they first learned that God is Spirit, it was through Him that their own spiritual life was heightened and that they became conscious of a Spirit surging into their own souls and they connected this whole wider manifestation of God with Him. They were right too in doing so. Christ's revelation of God had produced such spiritual effects upon them that they could now find Him within themselves, for God's spiritual presence in us is always proportioned to our capacity to have Him there. And then, too, they were now for the first time able to interpret that

which they felt within themselves. If
they found God, it was because they had
found Christ.

But they were right in a deeper sense.
If we think of the historical Christ, as I
have tried to set forth, as the manifestation of the Divine and the human in a
single personal Life then wherever man
finds God humanly revealed he properly
names the revelation with the historic
name. The historic incarnation was no
final event. It was the supreme instance
of God and man in a single life — the
type of continuous Divine-human fellowship. God's human revelation of Himself is not limited to a single date. As
Athanasius so boldly said: He became
man that we might become divine.
Christ is the prophesy of *a new humanity* — a humanity penetrated with the life

and power of God and this continued
personal manifestation of God through
men is Christ inwardly and spiritually
revealed.

It is a primary truth of Christianity
that God reaches man directly. No person is insulated. As ocean floods the
inlets, as sunlight environs the plant,
so God enfolds and enwreathes the finite
spirit. There is this difference, however, inlet and plant are penetrated
whether they will or not. Sea and sunshine crowd themselves in *a tergo*. Not
so with God. He can be received only
through appreciation and conscious ap-
propriation. He comes only through
doors that are *purposely* opened for
Him. A man may live as near God
as the bubble is to the ocean and yet not
find Him. He may be " closer than

breathing, nearer than hands or feet," and still be missed. Historical Christianity is dry and formal when it lacks the immediate and inward response to our Great Companion; but our spirits are trained to know Him, to appreciate Him, by the mediation of historical revelation. A person's spiritual life is always dwarfed when cut apart from history. Mysticism is empty unless it is enriched by outward and historical revelation. The supreme education of the soul comes through an intimate acquaintance with Jesus Christ of history. One who wished to feel the power of beauty would go to some supreme master of color and form who could exhibit them on canvas and not merely lecture about them. One who desired to feel the power of harmony would go, not to the boy with his harmonica, but to the Beethovens or Mozarts of the race who have revealed what an instrument and a human hand can do. So he who wishes to realize and practice the presence of God must inform himself at the source and fount, must come face to face with Him who was the highest human revelation of God. No one of us can interpret his own longings or purposes until he reads them off in the light of some loftier type of personality. That person understands himself best who grows intimate in fellowship with some noble character. And any man who wishes to discover the meaning of the inward voice and to interpret the divine breathings which come to human souls needs to be informed and illuminated by the supreme revelation of the ages.

With perfect fitness, then, we speak of

the inward Presence as the spiritual Christ. It is the continuation of the same revelation which was made under the " Syrian blue."

The procession of the Holy Ghost is a continuous revelation and exhibition of Christ within men. Whether we use the expression Holy Spirit or Christ within or spiritual Christ, we mean God *operating upon human spirits and consciously witnessed and appreciated in them.* " The Lord is the Spirit," cries Paul when, with unveiled face, he discovers that he is being transformed into His image from glory to glory. " Joined to the Lord in one Spirit," is another testimony of the same sort.

Unfortunately the doctrine of the Christ within — " the real presence "— has generally been held vaguely, and it has easily run into error and even fanaticism. The most common error has come from the prevalent view that when the Spirit — the inward Christ — comes in, the man goes out. It has been supposed that the finite is suppressed and the infinite supplants it and operates instead of it. This view is not only contrary to Scripture, but also contrary to psychological possibility. What really happens is that the human spirit through its awakened appreciation appropriates into its own life the divine Life which was always near and was always meant for it. The true view has been well put by August Sabatier[1]: " It is not enough to represent the Spirit of God as coming to the help of man's spirit, supplying strength which he lacks, an associate

[1] Sabatier, " Religions of Authority," p. 307.

or juxtaposed force, a supernatural aux-
iliary. Paul's thought has no room
for such a moral and psychological
dualism, although popular language easily permits it. His thought is quite
otherwise profound. There is no simple
addition of divine power and human
power in the Christian life. The Spirit
of God identifies itself with the human
me into which it enters and *whose life it
becomes*. If we may so speak, it is in-
dividualized in the new moral personality which it creates. A sort of meta-
morphosis, a transubstantiation, if the
word may be permitted, takes place in
the human being. Having been carnal
it has become spiritual. A " new man "
arises from the old man by the creative
act of the spirit of God. Paul calls
Christians πνευματικόι, properly speak-

4

ing, " the inspired." They are moved
and guided by the Spirit of God. The
spirit dwells in them as an immanent vir-
tue, whose fruits are organically devel-
oped as those of the flesh. Supernatural
gifts become natural, or rather, at this
mystical height, the antithesis created by
scholastic rationalism becomes meaningless and is obliterated." That is precisely my view and if I had not found
it here so well said I should have put
the same idea into my own words.
There are no known limits to the possible translation of the Spirit of God —
the Eternal Christ — into human personality. There are all degrees and
varieties of it as there are all degrees
and varieties of physical life. One
stands looking at a century-old oak tree
and he wonders how this marvelous thing

ever rose out of the dead earth where
its roots are. As a matter of fact it did
not. A tree is largely transformed sunlight. There is from first to last an
earth element to be sure, but the tree is
forever drawing upon the streams of sunlight which flood it and it builds the intangible light energy into leaf and blos-
som and fibre until there stands the old
monarch, actually living on sunshine!
But the little daisy at its feet, modest
and delicate, is equally consolidated sunshine, though it pushes its face hardly
six inches from the soil in which it was
born. So one spirit differs from another
spirit in glory. Some have but feebly
drawn upon the Spiritual Light out of
which strong lives are builded, others
have raised the unveiled face to the supreme Light and have translated it into

a life of spiritual beauty and moral fibre.
Thus the revelation of God in the flesh
goes on from age to age.   The Christ-
life propagates itself like all life-types —
the last Adam proves to be a life-giving
spirit.   He is the first born among many
brethren.   The actual re-creation, the
genuine identification of self with Christ
may go on until a man may even say —
" Christ lives in me; " " I bear in my
body the marks of the Lord Jesus; " " It
has pleased God to reveal His Son in
me."

" See if, for every finger of thy hands,
There be not found, that day the world
            shall end
Hundreds of souls, each holding by
            Christ's word,
That He will grow incorporate with all,

With me as Pamphylax, with him as
    John,
Groom for each bride! Can a mere man
    do this?
Yet Christ saith, this He lived and died
    to do.
Call Christ, then, the illimitable God."
I DO.

The Atonement

"Merely to repeat His words is not to continue His work; we must reproduce His life, passion and death. He desires to live again in each one of His disciples in order that He may continue to suffer, to bestow Himself, and to labor in and through them towards the redemption of humanity, until all prodigal and lost children be found and brought back to their Father's house. Thus it is that, instead of being removed far from human history, the life and death of Christ once more take their place in history, setting forth the law that governs it, and, by ceaselessly increasing the power of redemptive sacrifice, transform and govern it, and direct it towards its divine end."

Auguste Sabatier, " The Atonement," p. 134.

THE ATONEMENT.

IT is a bold and hazardous task to say anything on this subject and I must tread with bare, hushed feet, for it is a holy realm which we are essaying to enter. It must be understood from the first that I am not going to thresh over a heap of theological straw. I am not going into that realm of abstract metaphysics where one can always prove any thesis one may happen to assume at the start. I shall keep close to human experience. The pillars of our faith must be planted, not on some artificial construction of logic, but deep down in the actual experience of Life. There are external principles of the spiritual Life

which are as irresistible and compelling
as the laws of physics or the propositions
of Euclid. The task of the religious
teacher is to discover and proclaim these
elemental truths, but we always find it so
much easier to fall back on dogma and
theories which have been spun out of
men's heads! In the Gospels and in
Paul's letters the laboratory method prevails — the writers ground their asser-
tions on experienced facts, they tell what
they have found and verified, and they
always ask their readers to put their
truths to the test of a personal experience like their own. Our modern method must be a return to this inward laboratory method.

No one can carefully study the theories
of the atonement which have prevailed
at the various epochs of Christian history

without discovering that there has been in them a very large mixture of paganism. They have been deeply colored by mythology and by the crude ideas of primitive sacrifice. They start, not with the idea of God which Christ has revealed, but with a capricious sovereign, angry at sorely tempted, sinning man, and forgiving only after a sacrifice has satisfied Him. They treat sin not as a fact of experience, but as the result of an ancestral fall, which piled up an infinite debt against the race. They all move in the realm of law rather than in the domain of personality. They are all, more or less, vitiated by abstract and mathematical reasoning, while sin and salvation are always affairs of the inward life, and are of all things personal and concrete. The first step to a coercive conception of the atonement is to get out of the realm of legal phrases into the region of personality.

Sin is no abstract dogma. It is not a debt which somebody can pay and so wash off the slate. Sin is a fact within our lives. It is a condition of heart and will. There is no sin apart from a sinner. Wherever sin exists there is a conscious deviation from a standard — a sag of the nature, and it produces an effect upon the entire personality. The person who sins disobeys a sense of right. He falls below his vision of the good. He sees a path, but he does not walk in it. He hears a voice, but he says " no " instead of " yes." He is aware of a higher self which makes its appeal, but he lets the lower have the reins. There is no description of sin anywhere to com-

pare with the powerful narrative out of
the actual life of the Apostle Paul, found
in Romans VII: 9–25. The thing which
moves us as we read it is the picture here
drawn of our own state. A lower nature dominates us and spoils our life.
" What I would I do not; what I would
not that I do."

The most solemn fact of sin is its ac-
cumulation of consequences in the life of
the person. Each sin tends to produce
a *set* of the nature. It weaves a mesh
of habit. It makes toward a dominion,
or as Paul calls it, a *law of sin* in the
man —" Wretched Man," who sees a
shining possible life, but stays below,
chained to a body of sin. Sin, real sin,
and not the fictitious abstraction which
figures in theories, is a condition of personal will and action much more than a

debt to be paid or forgiven. The problem is far deeper. The only possible remedy here is to get a new man, a transformation of personality. Relief from *penalty* will not stead. Forgiveness is not enough. Relief from *penalty*, forgiveness alone, might spoil us, and make us think too lightly of our own sin.   No, it is not a judicial relief which our panting, sin-defeated hearts cry out for. We want more than the knowledge that the past is covered and will not count on the books against us. We want blackness replaced by whiteness, we want weakness replaced by power, we want to experience a new set of our innermost nature which will make us more than conquerors. We seek deliverance not from penalty and debt — but deliverance from the life of sin into a life of holy will.

There is still another aspect to sin which must be considered before we can fully appreciate the way of salvation which the Gospel reveals. Sin not only spoils the sinner's life and drags him into slavery. It separates him from God. It opens a chasm between him and his heavenly Father, or to vary the figure it casts a shadow on God's face. God seems far away and stern. The sense of warmth and tenderness vanishes. The sinner can see God only through the veil of his sins. This is a universal experience. The same thing happens in our relations with men. As soon as we have injured a person, treated him unfairly, played him false, a chasm opens between our life and his. We transfer

our changed attitude to him.   We dislike
to meet him.   We have no comfort in
his presence.   We interpret all his ac-
tions through the shadow which our deed
has created.   Our sense of wrong-doing
makes us afraid of the person wronged.

The conduct of little children offers
a good illustration of this subjective effect of sin, because in them one catches
the attitude at its primitive stage before
reflection colors it.   Some little child
has disobeyed his father and discovers,
perhaps for the first time, that he has
" something inside which he cannot do
what he wants to with," as a little boy
said.   When he begins to think of meeting his father he grows uncomfortable.
It is not punishment he is afraid of, he
has no anticipation of that.   He is conscious of wrong doing and it has made

a chasm between himself and his father. He reads his father's attitude now in the shadow of his deed. He has no joy or confidence in meeting him. Something strange has come between them.

What does the little fellow do? He instinctively feels the need of some sacrifice. He must soften his father by giving him something. He breaks open his bank and brings his father his pennies, or he brings in his hand the most precious plaything he owns, and acts out his troubled inward condition. He wants the gap closed and he feels that it will cost something to get it closed.[1]

---

[1] I am aware that this feature of child life will seem to some of my readers to be overdrawn. Some Mothers say that no such tendency was observed in their own children. That is quite likely. All children do not express their subtle and complex emotions in the same way. I do

That is human nature. That feeling is deep-rooted in man wherever he is found. He is conscious that sin separates and he feels that something costly and precious is required to close the chasm. Sacrifice is one of the deepest and most permanent facts of the budding spiritual life. Its origin is far back in history. The tattered papyrus, the fragment of baked clay, the pictorial inscription of the most primitive sort, all bear witness to this immemorial custom. It is as old as smiling or weeping, as hard to trace to a beginning as loving or hating. It is bound up with man's sense of guilt,

not mean to imply that every child *expresses* a need of sacrifice when he does wrong. But careful observers of children have frequently noted the facts which I have emphasized in the text, and I have often met them in my own experience with children.

and was born when conscience was born.
Dark and fantastic are many of the chap-
ters of the long story of man's efforts
to square the account. Priests have
seized upon this instinctive tendency and
have twisted it into abnormal shapes, but
they did not create it — it is elemental.
The idea of an angry God who must be
appeased and satisfied was born with
this consciousness of guilt, it is a natural
product of the shadow of human sin.[1]

---

[1] It has been shown by Robertson Smith and
others that the Hebrews thought of sacrifice not
as a gift to appease Jehovah but as a sharing of
a common meal with him. Such a lofty view of
sacrifice is surely not primitive. When sacrifice
had come to be thought of, as of a common meal,
it had already been purified and transformed by
centuries of development and the heightening
presupposes a series of unnamed prophets before
the list of great revealers whose names we know.
In the earliest stages religion is only very slightly
ethical. The moralization of religion is one of
the most tremendous facts of human history.

The historic theories of the atonement, inherited from the Roman church, were all formulated under the sway of this idea.

The two fundamental aspects of sin, then, are (1) its inward moral effect upon the soul, its enslaving power over the sinner, and (2) its tendency to open a chasm between God and man, to make God appear full of wrath. How does Christ meet this human situation? What is the heart of the Gospel? First of all, Christ reverses the entire pagan attitude. He reveals God as a Father whose very inherent nature is love and tenderness and forgiveness. In place of a sovereign demanding justice, He shows an infinite Lover. We must either give up the parable of the Prodigal Son, or accept this view of God. But this parable fits the entire Gospel. John was only uttering what Jesus Christ taught by every act of His life and what He exhibited supremely on His cross, when He said "God is Love." To surrender this truth, and to start with the assumption of a God who must be appeased, or reconciled or changed in attitude is to surrender the heart of the Gospel, and to weave the shining threads of our message of salvation in with the black threads of a pagan warp. He who came to show us the Father, has unmistakably showed Him full of love, not only for the saint, for the actual son; but also for the sinner, the potential son. Either God *is* Love, or we must conclude that Christ has not revealed Him as He is.

But the great difficulty is that so many fail to see what Divine Love and human

sin involve when they come together.   It
has superficially been assumed that if
God is a loving Father He will lightly
overlook sin and cannot be hard upon
the sinner.   They catch at a soft view of
sin and patch up a rose water theory of
its cure.   This soft view has appealed to
those who like an easy religion, and it
has often driven the evangelical Christian to an opposite extreme, which finds
no support in the Gospel.   To arrive at
a deeper view we must go back to Christ
and go down into the deeps of love as
we know it in actual human life.

True love is never weak and thin, and
unconcerned about the character of the
beloved.   The father does not " lay
aside " his love when he punishes his
erring boy, and keeps him impressed with
the reality of moral distinctions.   It is

the father's intense love which wields the rod. All true corrections and chastisements flow out of love. Even Dante knew this, when he wrote on the door of Hell, "Love was my maker." It is an ignorant and mushy love that cannot rise above kisses and sugar plums, and it is extremely superficial to set up a schism between love and justice.

But that is not all. Love always involves vicarious suffering. Love is an organic principle. It carries with it the necessity of sharing life with other persons, and in a world of imperfect persons, it means not only sharing gains and triumphs, it means, too, sharing losses and defeats. No man can sin in a sin-tight compartment. Suffer for his own sin the sinner assuredly will. But he does not stop there. Many innocent persons will suffer for it, too. This is one of the tragic aspects of life which has baffled many a lone sufferer like Job. Those who are nearest and closest to the sufferer will suffer most, but his sin has endless possibilities of causing suffering upon persons far remote in time and space. That ancient figure of the ripples from the little pebble, which sends rings to the farthest shores of the sea, is not overdrawn. Not one of us can estimate the havoc of his sin, or forecast the trail of suffering which it will leave behind it. So long as life remains organic there will be vicarious suffering.

But that is only one side of life. Holiness also involves a like suffering. There are no holiness-tight compartments. No man can be holy unto himself. Just as far as he has any rag of holiness he must share it — he must feel himself a debtor to others who lack — he must take up the task of making others holy.   *That costs something.*

You cannot command or compel people into holiness, you cannot increase their spiritual stature one cubit by any kind of force or compulsion.   You can do it only by sharing your life with them, by making them feel your goodness, by your love and sacrifice for them.   When a martyr dies for some truth, men suddenly discover for the first time how much it is worth and they eagerly pursue it over all obstacles.   In spiritual things we always make our appeal to the *cost* of the truth or the principle.   Think of the blood which has been shed for freedom of conscience!   Remember what a price has been paid in blood for the principle of democracy! Thus we speak of all the privileges of life. They are ours because somebody has felt that they were worth the cost, because somebody has died that we might freely have them. It is the tragedy of human life that we must suffer through the sin of others, and we must suffer also if we would carry goodness or holiness into other lives. Every bit of goodness which ever prevails anywhere in this world has cost somebody something.

This principle of vicarious suffering is no late arrival; it appears at every scale of life, heightening as we go up — becoming less blind and more voluntary. It was a central truth of Christ's revelation that this principle does not stop with man; it goes on up to the top of the spiritual scale. It finds its complete and

final expression in God Himself.   God's
life and our lives are bound together, as
a vine with branches, as a body with
members.   *So corporate* are we that no
one can give a cup of cold water to the
least person in the world without giving
it to Him!   But He is perfect and we
are imperfect, He is holy and we sin.
If the wayward boy, who wastes his life,
pains the heart of his mother whose life
is wrapped up in him, can we fling our
lives away and not make our Heavenly
Father suffer?   The cross is the answer.
He has undertaken to make Sons of God
out of such creatures as we are, to take
us out of the pit and the miry clay, to
put spiritual songs in our mouths and
write His own name on our foreheads,
will that cost Him nothing?   Again, the
cross is the answer.

Here we discover — it is the main miracle of the Gospel — that the original movement to bridge the chasm comes from the Divine side.   What man hoped to do, but could not, with his bleating lamb and timid dove, God Himself has done.   He has reached across the chasm, taking on Himself the sacrifice and cost, to show the sinner that the only obstruction to peace and reconciliation is in the sinner himself.   " This is love, not that we loved Him, but that He loved us," and this is sacrifice, not that we give our bulls and goats to please Him, but that He gives Himself to draw us.

Browning puts it all in a line:

" Thou needs must love me who have
    died for thee."

This is the key to Paul's great message

which won the Roman Empire. It was not a new philosophy. It was the irresistible appeal to love, exhibited in Christ crucified. "He loved me and gave Himself for me;" "We are more than conquerors through Him that loved us." "I am persuaded that neither death, nor life, nor angels, nor principalities, nor powers, nor things present, nor things to come, nor height, nor depth, nor any other created thing, shall be able to separate us from the *love of God,* which is in Christ Jesus our Lord." Sacrificing love, the Divine Heart suffering over sin, God Himself taking up the infinite burden and cost of raising men like us into sons of God like Himself; this is the revelation in the face of Jesus Christ. The heart that can stand *that* untouched can stand anything.

The power unto salvation, the dynamic
of the Gospel is in the cross, which ex-
hibits in temporal setting the eternal fact,
that God suffers over sin, that He takes
upon Himself the cost of winning sons
to glory and that His love reaches out to
the most sin-scarred wanderer, who
clutches the swine husks in his lean
hands.

But the appeal of love and sacrifice is
not the whole of the truth which this
word atonement covers.   We have been
seeing, in some feeble way, how God in
Christ enters into human life, identifies
Himself with us, and reveals the *energy
of Grace*.   But we cannot stop with
" what has been done for us without us."
Sin, as has been already said, is an affair
of personal choice — it is a condition of
inward life.   It is not an abstract entity,

in a metaphysical realm. It is the attitude of heart and will in a living, throbbing person who cannot get free from the
lower nature in himself. So too with
Salvation. It cannot be a *transaction* in
some realm foreign to the individual himself. It is not a plan, or scheme. It is
an actual deliverance, a new creation.
It is nothing short of a redeemed inward
nature. Such a change cannot be
wrought without the man himself. It
cannot come by *a tergo* compulsion. It
must be by a positive winning of the will.
A dynamic faith in the man must cooper-
ate with that energy from God. Something comes down from above, but something must also go up from below. Paul,
who has given the most vital interpreta-
tion of both sides of the truth of redemption — the objective and the sub-

jective — that has ever been expressed, uses the word " faith " to name the human part of the process.

Faith, in Paul's sense of it, means an identification of ourselves with Christ, by which we re-live His life. As He identified Himself with sinning humanity, so, by the attraction of his love, we identify ourselves with His victorious Life. We go down into death with Him — a death to sin and the old self — and we rise with Him into newness of life, to live henceforth unto Him who loved us.

There is no easy road out of a nature of sin into a holy nature. It is vain to try and patch up a scheme which will relieve us of our share of the tragedy of sin — or to put it another way, the travail for the birth of the sons of God. The Redeemer suffers, but He does not

suffer in our stead — He suffers in our
behalf, [ὑπέρ not ἀντι]. He makes His
appeal of love to us to share His life
as He shares ours. It is Paul's goal
— a flying goal, surely —" to know Him
and the power of His resurrection, and
the fellowship of His sufferings, being
made conformable unto His death."
The boldest word which comes from his
pen was: " I rejoice in my sufferings *on
your behalf;* and fill up that which is
lacking of the afflictions of Christ *in my
flesh,* for His body's sake, which is the
Church." (Col. 1, 24.) It is not re-
peating His words that saves us, it is re-
living His life, co-dying, and co-rising
with Him, and entering with a radiant
joy, caught from His face, into the common task of redeeming a world of sin to
a kingdom of love and holiness.

6

In that great book of spiritual symbolism — the Book of Revelation — those who overcome are builded, as pillars, into the Temple of God, and He writes His new name upon them. The new name is Redeemer. Those who have come up through great tribulation and have washed their robes in the blood of the Lamb are builded in as a permanent part of the Temple, where God reveals Himself, and they share with Him in the great redeeming work of the ages.

Whatever it has meant in the past, in the ages when the races were sloughing off their paganism, in the future the atonement must be vital and dynamic. It must be put in language which grips the heart, convinces the mind, and carries the will. It will name for us the Divine-human travail for a redeemed hu-

manity. It will cease to signify a way
by which God was appeased and it will
come to express, as it did in the apostolic
days, the identification of God with us in
the person of Christ, and the identification, by the power of His love, of ourselves with Him. We shall pass from
the terms which were inherited from
magic and ancient sacerdotal rites and
we shall use instead the language of our
riper experience. We shall abandon
illustrations drawn from law courts and
judicial decisions and we shall rise to
conceptions which fit the actual facts of
inward, personal experience where higher
and lower natures contend for the mas-
tery. The drama will not be in some
foreign realm, apart from human consciousness, it will rise in our thought into
the supreme drama of history — the

tragedy of the spiritual universe — the
battle of holiness with sin — the blood
and tears which tell the cost of sin and
create in response a passion for the Divine Lover who is our Father.   It will
stop at no fictitious righteousness which
is counted unto us, as though it were
ours.   We shall demand an actual redemption of the entire self which has become righteous, because it lives, in
Christ's power, the life which He lived.

We shall learn to tell the story in such
a way that the cross will not seem to be
brought in, as an afterthought, to repair
the damage wrought by an unforeseen
catastrophe.   It will stand as the consum-
mation of an elemental spiritual movement and it will be organic with the entire process of the making of men.
With charm and power, Ruskin has told

how the black dirt that soils the city pavement is composed of four elements which make, when they follow the law of their nature, the sapphire, the opal, the diamond and the dew drop. The glory and splendor do not appear in the black dirt, but the possibilities are there. When the law of the nature of these elements has full sweep the glory comes out. Man was not meant for a sinner, and to live a dark, chaotic life. There are far other possibilities in him. He is a potential child of God. The full nature has broken forth in one life and men beheld its glory. " To as many as receive Him, to them gives He power to become the sons of God."

Prayer

By prayer, I do not mean any bodily exercise of the outward man; but *the going forth of the spirit of Life towards the Fountain of Life, for fullness and satisfaction: The natural tendency of the poor, rent, derived spirit, towards the Fountain of Spirits.*

Isaac Penington.

"I, that still pray at morning and at eve,
Loving those roots that feed us from the past,
And prizing more than Plato things I learned
At that best Academe, a mother's knee,
Thrice in my life perhaps have truly prayed,
Thrice, stirred below my conscious self, have felt
That perfect disenthralment which is God."

Lowell's " Cathedral."

"The aim of prayer is to attain to the habit of goodness, so as no longer merely to have the things that are good, but rather to be good."

Clement of Alexandria.

PRAYER.

WE come now to the human search for a divine fellowship and companionship. Its complete history would be the whole story of religion. In this little book I shall speak only of certain definite human ways of seeking fellowship with God, namely, of prayer.

Prayer is an extraordinary act. The eyes close, the face lights up, the body is moved with feeling, and (it may be in the presence of a multitude) the person praying talks in perfect confidence with somebody, invisible and intangible, and who articulates no single word of response. It is astonishing. And yet it is a human custom as old as marriage, as ancient as grave-making, older than any city on the globe. There is no human activity which so stubbornly resists being reduced to a bread and butter basis. Men have tried to explain the origin of prayer by the straits of physical hunger, but it will no more fit into utilitarian systems than joy over beauty will. It is an elemental and unique attitude of the soul and it will not be " explained " until we fathom the origin of the soul itself!

But is not the advance of science making prayer impossible? In unscientific ages the universe presented no rigid order. It was easy to believe that the ordinary course of material processes might be altered or reversed. The world was conceived as full of invisible beings who could affect the course of events at will, while above all, there was a Being who might interfere with things at any moment, in any way.

Our world to-day is not so conceived. Our universe is organized and linked. Every event is *caused*. Caprice is banished. There is no such thing in the physical world as an uncaused event. If we met a person who told us that he had seen a train of cars drawn along with no couplings and held together by the mutual affection of the passengers in the different cars we should know that he was an escaped lunatic and we should go on pinning our faith to couplings as before. Even the weather is no more capricious than the course of a planet in space. Every change of wind and the course of every flying cloud is determined by previous conditions. Complex these combinations of circumstances certainly are, but if the weather man could get data enough he could foretell the storm, the rain, the drought exactly as well as the astronomer can foretell the eclipse. There is no little demon, there is no tall, bright angel, who holds back the shower or who pushes the cloud before him; no being, good or bad, who will capriciously alter the march of molecules because it suits our fancy to ask that the chain of causes be interrupted. What is true of the weather is true in every physical realm. Our universe has no caprice in it. Every thing is linked, and the forked lightning never consults our preferences, nor do cyclones travel exclusively where bad men live. As of old the rain falls on just and unjust alike, on saint and sinner. The knowledge of this iron situation has had a desolating effect upon many minds. The heavens have become as brass and the earth bars of iron. To ask for the interruption of the march of atoms seems to the scientific thinker the absurdest of delusions and all fanes of prayer appear fruitless. Others resort to the faith that there are " gaps " in the causal system and that in these unorganized regions — the domains so far unexplored — there are realms for miracle and divine wonder. The supernatural, on this theory is to be found out beyond the region of the " natural," and forcing itself through the " gaps." Those of this faith are filled with dread as they see the so called " gaps " closing, somewhat as the pious Greek dreaded to see Olympus climbed.

There are still others who evade the

difficulty by holding that God has made the universe, is the Author of its " laws," is Omnipotent and therefore can change them at Will, or can admit exceptions in their operation.   This view is well illustrated in the faith of George Müller, who writes: " When I lose such a thing as a key, I ask the Lord to direct me to it, and I look for an answer; when a person with whom I have made an appointment does not come, according to the fixed time, and I begin to be inconvenienced by it, I ask the Lord to be pleased to hasten him to me, and I look for an answer; when I do not understand a passage of the word of God, I lift up my heart to the Lord that He would be pleased by His Holy Spirit to instruct me, and I expect to be taught."

This view takes us back once more

into a world of caprice. It introduces a world in which almost anything may happen. We can no longer calculate upon anything with assurance. Even our *speed*, as we walk, is regulated by the capricious wish of our friends. But that is not all, it is a low, crude view of God — a Being off above the world who makes " laws " like a modern legislator and again changes them to meet a new situation, who is after all only a bigger man in the sky busily moving and shifting the scenes of the time-drama as requests reach him.

None of these positions is tenable. The first is not, for prayer is a necessity to full life, and the other two are not, because they do not fairly face the facts which are forced upon those who accept scientific methods of search and of thought. This physical universe is a stubborn affair. It is not loose and adjustable, and worked, for our private convenience, by wires or strings at a central station. It is a world of order, a realm of discipline. It is our business to discover a possible line of march in the world *as it is,* to find how to triumph over obstacles and difficulty, if we meet them — not to resort to " shun pikes " or cries for " exception in our particular case."

The real difficulty is that our generation has been conceiving of prayer on too low a plane. Faith is not endangered by the advance of science. It is endangered by the stagnation of religious conceptions. If religion halts at some primitive level and science marches on to new conquests of course there will be difficulty. But let us not fetter science, let us rather *promote* religion. We need to rise to a truer view of God and to a loftier idea of prayer. It is another case of " leveling up." On the higher religious plane no collision between prayer and science will be found. There will be no sealing of the lips in the presence of the discovery that all is law.

The prayer which science *has* affected is the spurious kind of prayer, which can be reduced to a utilitarian, " bread and butter," basis. Most enlightened persons now are shocked to hear " patriotic " ministers asking God to direct the bullets of their country's army so as to kill their enemies in battle, and we all hesitate to use prayer for the attainment of low, selfish ends, but we need to

7

cleanse our sight still farther and rise above the conception of prayer as an easy means to a desired end.

It is a fact that there are *valid prayer effects* and there is plenty of experimental evidence to prove the *energy of prayer*. It is literally true that " more things are wrought by prayer than this world dreams of." There are no assignable bounds to the effects upon mind and body of the prayer of living faith. Some of those particular cases of George Müller's are quite within the range of experience. The prayer for the lost key may well produce a heightened energy of consciousness which pushes open a door into a deeper stratum of memory, and the man rises from his knees and goes to the spot where the key was put. So too with the passage of Scripture. No

doubt many a man has come back from
his closet where the turmoil of life was
hushed and where all the inward currents
set toward God, many of us I say, come
back with a new energy and with cleared
vision and we can grasp what before
eluded us, we can see farther into the
spiritual meaning of any of God's reve-
lations.   There is perhaps never a sweep
of the soul out into the wider regions of
the spiritual world which does not
heighten the powers of the person who
experiences it.   Profound changes in
physical condition, almost as profound
as the stigmata of St. Francis, have in
our own times followed the prayer of
faith and many of us in our daily prob-
lems and perplexities have seen the light
break through, as we prayed, and shine
out, like a search light, on some plain

path of duty or of service.   There is un-
mistakable evidence of incoming energy
from beyond the margin of what we usu-
ally call " ourselves."

We have not to do with a God who is
" off there " above the sky, who can deal
with us only through " the violation of
physical law."   We have instead a God
" in whom we live and move and are,"
whose Being opens into ours, and ours
into His, who is the very Life of our
lives, the matrix of our personality; and
there is no separation between us unless
we make it ourselves.   No man, scien-
tist or layman, knows where the curve is
to be drawn about the personal " self."
No man can say with authority that the
circulation of Divine currents into the
soul's inward life is impossible.   On
the contrary, Energy does come in.   In

our highest moments we find ourselves in contact with wider spiritual Life than belongs to our normal *me*.

But true prayer is something higher. It is immediate spiritual fellowship. Even if science could demonstrate that prayer could never effect any kind of utilitarian results, still prayer on its loftier side would remain untouched, and persons of spiritual reach would go on praying as before. If we could say nothing more we could at least affirm that prayer, like faith, is itself the victory. The seeking is the finding. The wrestling is the blessing. It is no more a means to something else than love is. It is an end in itself. It is its own excuse for being. It is a kind of first fruit of the mystical nature of personality. The edge of the self is always touching a circle of life beyond itself to which it responds. The human heart is sensitive to God as the retina is to light waves. The soul possesses a native yearning for intercourse and companionship which takes it to God as naturally as the home instinct of the pigeon takes it to the place of its birth. There is in every normal soul a spontaneous outreach, a free play of spirit which gives it onward yearning of unstilled desire.

It is no mere subjective instinct — no blind outreach. If it met no response, no answer, it would soon be weeded out of the race. It would shrivel like the functionless organ. We could not long continue to pray in faith if we lost the assurance that there is a Person who cares, and who actually corresponds with us. Prayer has stood the test of experience. In fact the very desire to pray is in itself prophetic of a heavenly Friend. A subjective need always carries an implication of an objective stimulus which has provoked the need. There is no hunger, as Fiske has well shown, for anything not tasted, there is no search for anything which is not in the environment, for the environment has always produced the appetite. So this native need of the soul rose out of the divine origin of the soul, and it has steadily verified itself as a safe guide to reality.

What is at first a vague life-activity and spontaneous outreach of inward energy — a feeling after companionship — remains in many persons vague to the end. But in others it frequently rises to a definite consciousness of a personal Presence and there comes back into

the soul a compelling evidence of a real
Other Self who meets all the Soul's need.
For such persons prayer is the way to
fullness of life. It is as natural as
breathing. It is as normal an operation
as appreciation of beauty, or the pursuit
of truth. The soul is made that way,
and as long as men are made with mystical deeps within, unsatisfied with the
finite and incomplete, they will pray and
be refreshed.

Vague and formless, in some degree,
communion would always be, I think,
apart from the personal manifestation of
God in Jesus Christ. As soon as God
is known as Father, as soon as we turn
to Him as identical in being with our
own humanity, as suffering with us and
loving us even in our imperfection, this
communion grows defined and becomes

actual social fellowship which is prayer at its best. Paul's great prayers of fellowship rise to the God and Father of our Lord Jesus Christ, the God whom we know, because He has been humanly revealed in a way that fits our life. We turn to Him as the completeness and reality of all we want to be, the other Self whom we have always sought. The vague impulse to reach beyond our isolated and solitary self gives place to an actual experience of relationship with a personal Friend and Companion and this experience may become, and often does become, the loftiest and most joyous activity of life. The soul is never at its best until it enjoys God, and prays out of sheer love. Nobody who has learned to pray in this deeper way and whose prayer is a prayer of communion and fel-

lowship, wants logical argument for the
existence of God.   Such a want implies
a fall from a higher to a lower level.
It is like a demand for a proof of the
beauty one feels, or an evidence of love
other than the evidence of its experience.

Prayer will always rise or fall with
the quality of one's faith, like the mer-
cury in the tube which feels at once the
change of pressure in the atmosphere.
It is only out of *live faith* that a living
prayer springs.   When a man's praying
sinks into words, words, words, it means
that he is trying to get along with a dead
conception of God.   The circuit no
longer closes.   He cannot heighten his
prayer by raising his voice.   What he
needs is a new revelation of the reality
of God.   He needs to have the fresh
sap of living faith in God push off the

dead leaves of an outgrown belief, so that once more prayer shall break forth as naturally as buds in spring.

The conception of God as a lonely Sovereign, complete in Himself and infinitely separated from us " poor worms of the dust," grasshoppers chirping our brief hour in the sun, is in the main a dead notion. Prayer to such a God would not be easy with our modern ideas of the universe. It would be as difficult to believe in its efficiency as it would be to believe in the miracle of transubstantiation in bread and wine. But that whole conception is being supplanted by a *live faith* in an Infinite Person who is corporate with our lives, from whom we have sprung, in whom we live, as far as we spiritually do live, who needs us as we need him, and who is sharing with us the travail and the tragedy as well as the glory and the joy of bringing forth sons of God.

In such a kingdom — an organic fellowship of interrelated persons — prayer is as normal an activity as gravitation is in a world of matter. Personal spirits experience spiritual gravitation, soul reaches after soul, hearts draw toward each other. We are no longer in the net of blind fate, in the realm of impersonal force, we are in a love-system where the aspiration of one member heightens the entire group, and the need of one — even the least — draws upon the resources of the whole — even the Infinite. We are in actual Divine-human fellowship.

The only obstacle to effectual praying, in this world of spiritual fellowship, would be individual selfishness. To want to get just for one's own self, to ask for something which brings loss and injury to others, would be to sever one's self from the source of blessings, and to lose not only the thing sought but to lose, as well, one's very self.

This principle is true anywhere, even in ordinary human friendship. It is true too, in art and in music. The artist may not force some personal caprice into his creation. He must make himself the organ of a universal reality which is beautiful not simply for this man or that, but for man as man. If there is, as I believe, an *inner kingdom of spirit,* a kingdom of love and fellowship, then it is a fact that a tiny being like one of us can impress and influence the Divine Heart, and we can make our personal contribution to the Will of the universe, but we can do it only by wanting what everybody can share and by seeking blessings which have a universal implication.

So far as prayer is real fellowship, it gives as well as receives. The person who wants to receive God must first bring himself. If He misses us, we miss Him. He is Spirit, and consequently He is found only through true and genuine spiritual activity. In this correspondence of fellowship there is no more "violation of natural law" than there is in love wherever it appears. Love is itself the principle of the spiritual universe, as gravitation is of the physical; and as in the gravitate system the earth rises to meet the ball of the child, without *breaking any law*, so God comes to meet and to heighten the life of anyone who stretches up toward Him in appreciation, and there is joy above as well as below.

All that I have said, and much more, gets vivid illustration in the "Lord's prayer," which Christians have taken as a model form, though they have not always penetrated its spirit.   It is in every line a prayer of fellowship and co-operation.   It is a perfect illustration of the social nature of prayer.   The co-operation and fellowship are not here confined, and they never are except in the lower stages, to the inward communion of an individual and his God.   There is no *I* or *me* or *mine* in the whole prayer.   The person who prays spiritually is enmeshed in a *living group* and the reality of his vital union with persons like himself clarifies his vision of that deeper Reality to whom he prays. Divine Fatherhood and human brotherhood are born together.   To say Father to God involves saying " brother " to one's fellows, and the ground swell of either relationship naturally carries the other with it, for no one can largely realize the significance of brotherly love without going to Him in whom love is completed.

" Hallowed be thy name " is often taken in a very feeble sense to mean " keep us from using thy name in vain," or it is thought of as synonymous with the easy and meaningless platitude, " Let thy name be holy."   It is in reality a heart-cry for a full appreciation of the meaning of the Divine name, i. e., the Divine character.   It is an uprising of the soul to an apprehension of the holi-

ness of God and the fullness of His life
that the soul may return to its tasks with
a sense of infinite resources and under
the sway of a vision of the true ideal.
This Lord's prayer begins with a word
of intimate relationship and social union
—" Our Father." It then goes out beyond the familiar boundaries of experience to feel the infinite sweep of God's
completeness and perfectness and to become penetrated with solemn awe and
reverence which fit such companionship,
—" Our Father of the holy name."

This is the prelude. The true melody
of prayer, if I may say so, begins with
the positive facing of the task of life:—
" Thy kingdom come, Thy will be done
on earth as it is in heaven." Here again
we have the loftiest Fellowship. The
person who prays this way is linked with

8

God in one mighty spiritual whole. The last vestige of atomic selfishness is washed out. There are those who say these words of prayer with folded hands and closed eyes, and then expect the desired kingdom to come by miracle; they suppose that if the request is made often enough a millennium age will drop out of the skies. Ah, no! If God is Spirit and man is meant to be spiritual, such a millennium is a sheer impossibility. This prayer involves the most strenuous life that ever was lived. To pray seriously for the coming of the kingdom of heaven means to contribute to its coming. It *has* come in any life which is completely under the sway of the holy Will and which is consecrated to the task of making that holy Will prevail in soci-

ety.   It is no " far off Divine event."
It is always coming.

> " For an ye heard a music, like enow
> They are building still, seeing the city
>   is built
> To music, therefore never built at all
> And therefore built forever."

In a plain word, it is the total task of
humanity through the ages.   It is the
embodiment in a temporal order of the
eternal purpose.   It is the weaving in
concrete figure and color of the Divine
pattern.   It is the slow and somewhat
painful work of making an actual Divine
society out of this rather stubborn and
unpromising potential material.   But it
is our main business, and this prayer is
the girding of the loins for the sublime
task of helping God make His world.

" Man as yet is being made, and e'er the
    crowning age of ages,
Shall not aeon after aeon pass and touch
    him into shape?
All about him shadow still, but, while
    the races flower and fade,
Prophet eyes may catch a glory, slowly
    gaining on the shade,
Till the people all are one and all their
    voices blend in a choric
Hallelujah to the Maker, ' It is finished;
    man is made.' "

Fellow laborers with God in truth we
are. Prayer ends in labor and labor
ends in prayer. But it is not a cry for
miracle. It is an inward effort at co-
operation.

There is a beautiful mingling of the
great and the little, the cosmic and the

personal. The universal sweep of Divine ends does not swallow up, or miss, the needs of the concrete individual. While the spiritual universe is building, men must have daily bread and they must constantly face the actual present with its routine and monotony. Here again prayer is no miraculous method of turning stones into bread. It is no easy substitute for toil. It is the joyous insight that in the avenues of daily toil, God and man are co-operating and that in very truth the bread for the day is as much God given as it is won by the sweat of brow. The recently discovered "saying of Jesus" best interprets this prayer. "Wherever any man raises a stone or splits wood, there am I." He consecrates honest toil.

Next we come to the profound word

which shows how completely our lives
are bound together in organic union,
above and below: "Forgive us as we
forgive." What a solemn thing to say.
Dare we pray it! And yet few words
have ever so truly revealed the nature
of prayer. It is, one sees, no easy, lazy
way to blessings. Once more, it is co-
operation. "Forgiveness is not a gift
which can fall upon us from the skies,
in return for a capricious request. The
blessing depends on us as much as it
does on God. A cold, hard, unforgiv-
ing heart can no more be forgiven than a
lazy, slipshod student can have knowledge given to him. Like all spiritual
things, forgiveness can come only when
there is a person who appreciates its
worth and meaning. The deep cry for
forgiveness must rise out of a forgiving

spirit. It is always more than a transaction, an event. It is an inward condition of the personal life, and the soul
that feels what it means to love and forgive is so bound into the whole divine
order that love and forgiveness come in
as naturally as light goes through the
open casement, or the tide into an inlet.

The next word is surely to be thought
of as a human cry: "Take us not into
testing." It is the natural shrinking of
the tender, sensitive soul, and it is the
right attitude. Most of us know by
hard experience that trial, proving, testing, yes, even actual temptation, have a
marvelous ministry. No saint is made
in the level plain, where the waters are
still and the pastures green.

" Never on custom's oiléd grooves
   The world to a higher level moves,
   But grates and grinds with friction
     hard
   On granite boulder and flinty shard.
   The heart must bleed before it feels,
   The pool be troubled before it heals."

All this we know. We know that the stern battle makes the veteran. But this prayer is the childlike cry, the shrinking fear, which are always safer than the bold dash, the impetuous plunge. It is the utterance of an instinctive wish to keep where safety lies, and, humanly speaking, it is right, though, in a world whose highest fruit is character, we may expect that bitter cups and hard baptisms will be a part of our experience. Like all that has gone before, it is an

effort at co-operation. It is a sincere aspiration for green pastures and still
waters joined with a readiness to be fed
at the table in presence of the enemy, if
need be, readiness for the perilous edge
of conflict, for " high strife and glorious
hazard."

Last of all there rises the cry for deliverance from the power of evil. Once
more we realize that this is not an occasion for magical interference, no call
for a fiery dart out of the sky to pierce
a black demon who is pushing us into
sin. The drama is an inward one and
the enemy, called of many names, is a
part of our own self. Each soul has
its own struggle with the immemorial
tug of brute inheritance—the sag of
lower nature.

" When the fight begins within himself,
  A man's worth something. God
        stoops o'er his head,
Satan looks up between his feet — both
      tug —
He's left, himself, i' the middle: The
      soul wakes
  And grows."

But here supremely appears our principle of co-operation. Prayer for deliverance from evil cannot end on the lips. There is no conquest of the flesh, no killing out of ape and tiger, until we ourselves catch at God's skirts and rise to live for the Spirit and by the Spirit. There is no deliverance till the soul says, " I will be free " and God and man tug on the same side. Wherever any citadel of evil is battered God and man are there together. God finds a human organ and man draws on the inexhaustible resources of God.

Prayer, whether it be the lisp of a little child, or the wrestling of some great soul in desperate contest with the coils of habit or the evil customs of his generation is a testimony to a divine-human fellowship. In hours of crisis the soul feels for its Companion, by a natural gravitation, as the brook feels for the ocean. In times of joy and strength, it reaches out to its source of Life, as the plant does to the sun. And when it has learned the language of spiritual communion and knows its Father, praying refreshes it as the greeting of a friend refreshes one in a foreign land. We ought not to expect that prayer, of the true and lofty sort, could be attained by easy steps. It involves appreciation of God and co-operation with Him. One comes not to it in a day. Even human friendship is a great attainment. It calls for sacrifice of private wishes and for adjustment to the purposes of another life. One cannot be an artist or a musician without patient labor to make oneself an organ of the reality which he fain would express. He must bring himself by slow stages to a height of appreciation. Prayer is the highest human function. It is the utterance of an infinite friendship, the expression of our appreciation of that complete and perfect Person whom our soul has found. "Lord, teach us how to pray."